The Everyday Miracles

Michael Drury

THE EVERYDAY MIRACLES

A Woman's Views on Personal Fulfillment

 HALLMARK EDITIONS

ACKNOWLEDGMENTS: "Privacy, the Secret Side of Marriage." Copyright © Michael Drury 1968. "Guilt, the Poisoner of Love." Copyright © Michael Drury 1969. "Humility: The Misunderstood Virtue." Copyright © Michael Drury 1961. "The Other Side of Giving." Copyright © Michael Drury 1962. "What Do We Owe Our Parents?" Copyright © Michael Drury 1957. "What Is Maturity?" Copyright © Michael Drury 1958. "Success, Good or Bad?" Copyright © Michael Drury 1959. "Enthusiasm: The God Within." Copyright © Michael Drury 1960. "What's to Become of You?" Copyright © Michael Drury 1962. "The Beauty of Courage." Copyright © Michael Drury 1963. "Never Say Never." Copyright © Michael Drury 1964. "Welcome Yourself." Copyright © Michael Drury 1965. "The Women in My Life." Copyright © Michael Drury 1957. "The Courage to Grow and the Right to Fail." Copyright © Michael Drury 1965. "The Gifts of Solitude." Copyright © Michael Drury 1969. "What Have I Learned From Men?" Copyright © Michael Drury 1956. "What I Have Learned From Other People's Children." Copyright © Michael Drury 1964.

Contents

Learning to Be
A Woman

Being a female one cannot help; being a woman is an achievement. I didn't make that up. It was taught to me—by women.

In the small western town where I grew up, there lived two elderly sisters, Frenchwomen, one of them totally blind. Mademoiselle, the younger sister, the blind one, would offer me sweets and play French songs on the piano and show me old, brown photographs of their home in France. Madame, the older one, was a large woman with a prodigious bosom, smoldering brown eyes, a big straight nose, and an air of power.

It was years before I understood the spell those women cast over our whole town, each in her different way, and it was Madame herself who revealed it to me.

I went to pay them a final visit before going off to college, about equally divided between pride and dismay. I sat in Madame's kitchen. Madame spooned

apricots into a dish and poured cream over them . . .
her burning eyes were on me. "You have within you
the one secret. Don't you know that? To be a woman. I do not speak of female but of *woman*. A great
man is commonplace, but a great woman is rare and
priceless. Think of that and the rest will come."

She nodded, eyeing me with amusement and scorn
from her mountaintop of seventy-odd years. "Look
at you, yes. Look at me or my sister. Do you suppose
with this nose and that affliction we were in our
youth — oomph?" (Oomph was a word in those
days; it meant glamour, an aura, juices, electricity.)
She paused. Memories at which I couldn't even guess
momentarily held her tongue. "Ah, but we were
women. Know women, study them, learn from them,
and you will have lovers shooting themselves at dawn
for you if that is what you want. Most of all you
will have yourself." She poked my chest with a long
knotted finger. "Woman," she said. "Here."

The flower of femininity
To be a woman assuredly means more than just
not being a man. But what? This turns out to be a
curiously difficult question.

Much of what we deem masculine or feminine is
socially imposed. Historically, religiously, culturally,
male-and-female represent completion. I beseech
Western society not to forget that. At the same time,

I maintain vigorously woman's right to equality and recognition. Where, in such a position, is the root and flower of femininity?

A refugee woman who has spent more time than most people concretely searching for identity once said, "I am first of all man—that is, anthropologically, I am not beast—then woman, then daughter of such-and-such parents, then American, then a teacher, a Californian, resident of a given city, then a consumer, friend, driver, property-owner, occasional student and much else. Only after that, which I am and would be without marriage, am I Mrs. So-and-So, wife to a certain man, mother of certain children. I love the position but I endow it, it does not endow me."

Here is one answer to my question, for to feel oneself a woman and to equate that with being a person is the essence of what we value so highly, and rightly, as femininity. To combine these gracefully is the great contribution of our age. Women as a whole class are only beginning to esteem their femininity not as a substitute for personality, but equally with it.

What women have taught me

I have known many women—good and ordinary and a few the world called bad. In the degree that they were women—not just female—and in the measure of my readiness to listen, I have learned from them and been blessed. . . .

I have learned from women that I am a multi-level being, and that even in monotony or sorrow or dismay, there are fragmentary beauties all around me to make life worth living.

I once had a teacher who used to take us outside to lie in the spring grass and make lists of all the sounds we could hear, from the droning of insects to the shout of younger children at recess, from bird-calls to the shifting of gears in cars on the highway. My mother has a poet's eye and ear and nose for such small wonders. Not long ago I was helping a friend get dinner in her kitchen when she cut a dark red onion in half and we paused to admire its clean-ness and its design, sharing it, finding in it and in our mutual enjoyment of it a gleam of infinite won-der.

Women, indeed. I like them. They have given me, most of all, myself, as Madame promised they would so many years ago. It is men who mold what we do, but it is women who make us what we are. I am glad to be a woman and to be learning what that means.

Masculinity and Femininity

Last summer at a beach picnic, a man said, "Step aside, girls, this is man's work," when it came to building the fire, and he then concocted an excellent blaze. But I smiled, thinking of an Indian tribe I once spent some time with where any male would have perished from shame and embarrassment at having to perform so feminine a task as making a cooking fire. In fact, to do exactly that was one of the worst punishments the tribe could administer.

Because masculine and feminine traits are largely cultural does not argue that they are unreal or unimportant. We live in a culture, not in a vacuum. It is widely recognized that all human beings are a mixture, physically and mentally, of male and female qualities. Knowing this, and knowing their general cultural pattern, we can cultivate them and interchange them without damage, but, on the contrary, to our great enrichment.

The test of real love

I once heard a psychiatrist say we fall in love with the kinds of men we would be if we were male, or women we would be if we were female—in other words, the person who reflects our own other side, although we may do it instinctively without conscious knowledge that we have another side. Whether one agrees with this idea or not, it can be revealing to examine the men one is attracted to in light of it. I have used it sometimes with young people who ask how you know if you are really in love. "If you were a boy," I say to them, "would you be like him? Is he what you would want to be?" It can clarify the vision as nothing else does, and not always for the worse. Often it comforts and reassures.

Deeply trusted convictions

I go back to my original plea for man and woman as wholeness, a unit, which means simply and unqualifiedly, one. Man and woman exist largely, though not exclusively, in relation to each other; and one cannot be destructive to a portion of one's own nature without being destructive to oneself. Masculinity and femininity are deeply felt, deeply believed, deeply *trusted* convictions. The man or woman who has this inner faith has self-possession and attracts to it that which results in self-completeness.

Welcome Yourself

Do you really want yourself or would you like to exchange that self for some other you fancy—prettier or richer or more gifted or luckier or more loved? Many people are privately convinced they have been singled out for trouble, that they have it just a little harder than others. It is not so, and it is one of the most dangerous of delusions. It fritters away the energies that should go directly into the self you now are. You have what Dr. Edward Teller, the noted physicist, called "unused excellencies," which he said lie dormant in almost everyone. The continuing challenge to all of us is to want ourselves, our own excellencies, not somebody else's.

If you would appreciate yourself and enjoy yourself, you must do what is required to know another person: spend time with yourself. Be alone sometimes, and be silent. Retreat from the pattern and habit without and cultivate what is within.

Different kinds of alone

There are four kinds of alone, and each is needful, though some are more readily attained than others.

One is to be alone at home, in familiar surroundings but without demands, without turning to the radio or television to keep you company. What shall you do? I don't know. That is what you are alone for, to find out.

A second kind of aloneness is at large. Go to a museum or art gallery or concert or play or film or restaurant or just for a walk on busy streets—alone. React to the painting or performance, the street sounds and sights inside your own head, without trying to communicate it. Absorb, listen, look, ingest, reflect.

Third, there is traveling alone. Whether on a plane, a ship, or just a city bus; in a foreign country or only a different section of your own city—being alone in an alien situation is instructive. Don't be surprised if you find within a certain amount of panic. That is the point: to displace yourself so that you learn how much is you and how much is background.

And fourth, there is the intense aloneness of living for a time, hours or days or weeks, on sand dunes or in a forest or on an ice floe. Alone with the components of the universe, perhaps with God. This is, of course, the most drastic, the most powerful kind of alone. Few of us can do it often and many would not want to, but nobody who has ever really tried it is quite so alone again. He has met himself.

Where
The Love
of Others Begins

Can you imagine Abraham Lincoln declining to run for president on the grounds of its being vainglorious? Can you imagine Sir Winston Churchill, or Mrs. Eleanor Roosevelt, or St. Theresa, or Babe Ruth, or Charles Lindbergh, or Florence Nightingale, or Beethoven waiting around for somebody else to point out their paths or personalities? True, these people had particularity, but so have you.

Love of others begins in decent self-esteem. If you don't believe in your own entity, you can't very well give it to others in love, in work, in service or anything else. All great contributions have been made by women and men who, far from effacing the self, cherished and utilized it, commanded it, trained it, freed it, enjoyed it—yes, even the saints. Bitterness and defeat come from nonuse of our powers, stifled abilities, unrealized self.

The "Me in Me"

In Enid Bagnold's searching play, *The Chinese Prime Minister*, the leading character, who is seventy years old, says, "There is a me in me I have not conquered yet—or even found." This alludes to a deeply significant fact: that there is a self beyond the self—and for all we know, another and another —which must be satisfied if we are to live comfortably in our own skins. This is not abstract philosophy, though you can carry it to that, but brownbread reality. It is the "me in me" that mutters beneath the surface of our lives like an angry volcano: that asks of the "right" marriage, the house, the college education, the success, the children, the car, the clothes, the travel. Is that all? Is this what life is about? Life is found in movement, not in form. Art, including the art of living, is bringing order out of chaos, but the chaos has to be there as working substance or the order becomes flat, tasteless, hollow, barren.

The only way to achieve creative chaos is through commitment. Do something, master something, care about something, and submit constantly to correction. . . .

What Is Maturity?

Maturity is one of those words, like schizophrenic and sophistication, that have been used so loosely they flap. If you are mature, you are presumed to be happy, secure, married, well-liked and something called adjusted—or capable of becoming all these. If you aren't mature, you are either incorrigible, defective or warped and, in any case, heaven help you. Such dogma mistakes the outward appearance for the inward fact and betrays a passion for what maturity most decidedly is not—the proclivity to wrap life up in neatly labeled packages so that one need never bother about it again.

A maturity proper for every age

There is no such thing as being wholly mature. Maturity isn't a thing, it's a continuous development—and realizing that is a mark of maturity in itself. It is not the same experience for all people any more than love is, or happiness is, nor can it be measured by tapes and charts, nor does one arrive at it in some magical moment and stay there for the rest of his life. There is a maturity proper and possible to every age. Physical adulthood has very little to do with it.

Maturity always has somewhere to go and an eye and an ear for the million delights and interests en route. That's what it is in part—never feeling quite over with, washed up, done. It is as though a seed were to accept itself as a very fine, first-rate seed, yet knew it had a destiny to become a rose or a carrot or whatever kind of seed-nature it had, and *liked* the idea.

Maturity takes experience

It is logical enough to associate maturity with time because maturity takes experience and experience does not happen in a moment. Yet young people have, by their very inexperience, certain qualities that the adult must preserve if he would be mature.

For one thing, they're trusting; they are not suspicious by nature. For another, they're teachable, flexible, ready to try the new thing—a new hairdo, new jazz, a new attitude. Young people are always looking—for a mate, a job, a cause to believe in, adventure—and the result is an openness to experience, a willingness to be involved that is an important ingredient of maturity.

It is not age then but insight that promotes maturity. Dr. Bruno Walter, the famous conductor, said a wise and witty thing on the occasion of his eightieth birthday. "I feel," he said, "in no way older or younger than I ever did." Note that significant phrase *or younger* for it reveals a mature man, not by reason of his years but by independence of those years.

Signposts of maturity

What then is maturity? No one can say for all time to come, for, like infinity, if you could bottle it up in a definition it would cease to be itself. How can you be sure you're acquiring it? You can't—if you're looking for rules and formulas. Maturity isn't a destination, it's a road. It has, of course, some signposts. The more mature one becomes, the more he recognizes these experiences when they happen to him.

The moment when you wake up after some staggering blow—some grief or hurt or disappointment—and think, "I'm going to live after all." The moment when you find out something you have long believed isn't so. And the one after that when you have parted with the old conviction and find to your astonishment that you're still you. The moment you discover somebody can do your job as well as you can, and you go on doing it anyway. The moment you do the thing you've always been afraid of. The moment you realize you are forever alone but so is everybody else and so in some strange and wonderful way you are more together than ever. The moment you know life is a perpetual becoming. And a hundred thousand other moments, in which you find out who you are.

The
Gifts of
Solitude

No man or woman who does not know what it is to walk alone can truly walk with others. Men like Socrates and Jesus were good company and much invited out to dinner, but one thing that made them attractive was the time they spent apart, staying for long stretches. You may complain that you are not a Socrates, but all people have the same access to the same spirit in their degree. The most compelling people on earth are those who recognize and salute our uniqueness, our being somebody—and to be unique, one person and no other, is to be, in that measure, alone.

Enjoying everyday miracles
I like to go to the theater or a concert or a baseball

game by myself sometimes, just to have it all my own again—to renew that one-to-one skirmish that life always is in the beginning. When you first fall in love, or hear a Beethoven sonata, or learn to ski, or cook a trout, or watch the sunrise, or really see yourself through other eyes—and not only feel but *know* that it has never happened before, not in just this combination—that is joy. It exists between you and God, and need not be described or explained. It is happening to you, one lone human being, and therefore it is happening in the world.

One day a friend brought me three iris buds from her garden. They had not been on my desk twenty minutes when I looked up from my work to discover one had opened. Beguiled, I thought if it could happen that fast, I would watch the next one. I sat still and waited. The flower was shy, almost stubborn; there was at first nothing to be seen. Then slowly, gently, inexorably, the blue petals disengaged—an everyday miracle that made me hold my breath. At the last moment there was a suddenness, a quick final burst, and with it a sound, the softest imaginable *pub* as the petals pulled apart and the full-scale blossom unfurled, glorious, triumphant. I was not a little staggered.

Hardly a world-shaking event, and yet I was richer for it. One almost has to be alone to accommodate such things. . . .

Loneliness is frequently boredom

It would be foolish to deny that solitariness is sometimes somber and rough going. In such instances, the best recourse I know is not so much action as variation. What is called loneliness is frequently boredom.

Whatever your custom, try another. If you work primarily with your hands, do something with your head. If you habitually sit down, stand up. If you encounter mostly women, try men: teach rug-making in a veterans' hospital or dancing to plant workers. If you see only adults, try children: at the very least you can child-sit for a friend, but you can also work in a community center, Scout troop or children's theater. If nobody needs you, need somebody: hire a student to teach you French; invite someone to dinner, each of you contributing part of the meal, if necessary; get a knowledgeable friend to introduce you to an art museum.

A lot of this comes under the heading of doing unto others, I know, but there is a subtle advantage in not going at it that way. It keeps your expectations realistic. No effort of this kind is going to wipe out the solitary nature of existence now and forever.

Awareness that we are alone, like any other strong emotion, has something important to say to us. All we need to do is listen.

The Secret of Enthusiasm

Early one spring evening I walked down a busy New York street with a man who had been working fiercely hard. He needed a rest, but he seemed to draw on some inner well of energy and goodwill. Suddenly, he stopped and said, "I hear a cricket." Horns blew, feet hurried by, cars rumbled past, and that man's mind was groggy with an abstruse problem—yet he heard a cricket. We hunted till we found him, scraping his legs at the edge of a grating, and we smiled and went on oddly comforted, not by a bug exactly, but by being reminded of our own ability to perceive and receive a world. I learned then that enthusiasm is partly willing attention, a turning aside to see instead of hunching up inside like the affronted snail. Enthusiasm is what keeps us in touch with our world. Without it, we are blind and deaf and halt and only half-know it.

The god within and the art without

True adult enthusiasm is not puppy-dog eagerness for every new smell and sound and blade of grass, but rather the original endowment grown up— tempered and shaped by experience, judgment, humor. The word enthusiasm comes from *en-theos*—the god within—and means basically to be inspired or possessed by the god, or, if you like, by God. It is the open secret, as commonplace and tireless as sunlight, that gives joy and purpose to all our days, if only we don't despise it.

There is no magic formula that can cloak us with gladness in living. It comes from willingness to find one's own way—indeed, enthusiasm is that willingness. At times, this involves acceptance of things as they are; at others, it means daring to impose one's elbowroom all over creation.

Sometimes it is not one's business to change the world, and neither self-pity nor reproach is much aid to delight in what one is doing. Somewhere between wanting to make the world over and wanting to hide from it is a balance that permits intelligent adult enthusiasm. This god within becomes the art without, and we no longer beg to know what life means: we furnish the meaning by being.

A sanctuary in the hustle

Zest for daily living springs from a feeling of uniqueness, the intuitive sense of being a self. Identity is indispensable to pleasure in being alive. We are either something or we are nothing. To feel oneself a cipher will smother any spirit.

Enthusiasm is sustained by the free play of our faculties. It has been said that when a human being learns to read, his other senses atrophy, and even his vision is exercised as a utensil, rarely as a joy. But it isn't reading that does that; it's our fixed regard for utility. Thus, when crossing the street we see that there's a car coming and we go back to the curb. We need such information to survive, but it's only the footwork of sensibility and ought not to supplant that world beyond, where a yellow taxi on a rain-black pavement is transportation, yes, but also a streak of color across a gray day and a reason to have eyes.

A smell of pines or salty sea air or wet soil can bring us a memory ten thousand years old, and with it a sense of roots and timelessness. The shouts of children uncooped from school, the murmur of dragonflies along a river, the wheezing music of a merry-go-round—these things cool the mind and mend the heart if only for a moment. Hours are only moments added up, and they make a sanctuary in the hustle. I know no other way to make one.

Humility: Misunderstood Virtue

Few people know what humility is, and the rest of us are uneasy with what we think it may be. It seems vaguely desirable, but not really attractive. It may get one into heaven, but it won't promote a raise in pay. We suspect it is spineless, yet paradoxically credit it with power to drive out all else: brains, talent, energy, courage, delight—as though humility would not mix with complexity of intellect and a vigorous spirit.

Actually, the reverse is true. Those whom we commonly hail for their humility—Jesus, Socrates, Lincoln, Gandhi, Einstein—have never been timorous souls, but figures of strong destiny with a fierce determination to carry it out. The veery thrush wears a drab coat but that isn't all of him: his song is liquid silver. Humility should not saturate a character but flavor it. Humility is not being a doormat; it is a tough, free, confident characteristic.

The job of humility

Humility isn't self-disparagement; it is good judgment. It is the unstuffed shirt; the size-ten feet in size-ten shoes, not crammed into size-six; the grace to say "thank you" for recognition of a job well done, whether it is a good dinner or a rocket in orbit. It is patience.

One of the characters in Gilbert and Sullivan's *Ruddigore* laments, "You've no idea what a low opinion I have of myself and how little I deserve it." We laugh at him but our own sense of humility is often not much sharper.

My mother lives on a mountain where in summer the stars are as big as chrysanthemums and, to my city-trained eye, almost frighteningly close. One night some years ago as we stood under them, simply looking, I was moved by what I supposed was humility to say, "Doesn't it make you feel insignificant?"

"No," my mother said, "only grateful at being included in such a universe." There was amusement in her tone, and I saw that she was laughing gently at my fuzzy notion of humility, what it is and what it does for one. I realized that it is not the job of humility to make us feel small, but to expand our capacity for appreciation, awe, delight, to stand silent before all that we do not know—and then get on with the work of finding out.

Humility is necessary and useful for the same reason a lead keel is useful on a racing sloop: it keeps us from tipping over. It takes equanimity to view another's good and not be swayed off course either by envy or by admiration. The neighborhood child who is plainly superior and is not one's own child; the man who is elected company president when you were in line for it; the woman who got rich by marrying a rich man; the teammate who keeps walloping homers over the fence when you are in a slump—life is filled with such people, and it takes genuine humility to keep them in perspective, neither too high nor too low. Humility is poise.

A long lesson in humility

We should not expect total humility from ourselves or others any more than we expect total wisdom. It takes a working knowledge of who and what one is to be humble in the right times and places, and this requires experience, which in turn requires time. James S. Barrie once said, "Life is a long lesson in humility." We ought not to blame or be blamed for not mastering the art in three weeks.

Everyday Courage

Courage is democratic. Everybody has it in some measure, for it takes courage merely to stay alive. Courage is discovery: the exploring of a self you did not know was there. Courage is believing: touching bottom and using the touch to push yourself off again to the shining surface. The opposite of courage is not so much fear as laziness, indifference, discouragement, defeat, cynicism—*un*courage, so to speak. Fear is only an acute example of uncourage.

There is a workaday courage required of people, less spectacular but in some ways more exacting because it is endless and because it doesn't always look like courage.

The courage, for example, to keep your mouth shut when you know a fascinating bit of gossip. The courage to be pleasant but firm when you must make a complaint, or fire somebody, or take an article back to a store. The courage to vote with the minority at your school or church or club. The courage to put out a hand to the less popular girl, to be seen at a dance with the less attractive young man who asked you first. The courage to say no to a project too far out; to give a party although it scares you; to congratulate the girl who got promoted instead of you. The courage to make your own miracles, to find beauty in the ordinary, in the cliché: the heart of a flower, cucumber peelings on a cutting board, a baby's skin, late afternoon sunlight slanting across the city. The courage, in short, to live life strongly and not be lukewarm.

Courage is contagious. When other people exhibit it, we like them, because they widen and increase the meaning of our own humanity.

Courage is acceptance

Courage is often stubborn or sudden defiance; it is also acceptance when there is simply no alternative. It requires, too, a certain recklessness, since courage is action on incomplete information—which is a fairly accurate description of the continuing condition of life. Nobody has all the answers; nobody can see around corners. We don't fuss much about it, but keeping on is rather a brave thing to do.

The Bible says we were not given "the spirit of fear, but of power, of love and of a sound mind." Fear is ugly and defeat is repellent, but courage is comely because we are at home with it. It becomes us. As a fish is beautiful in water or a bird in flight, man too is lovely in his native elements—among them courage.

The Other Side of Giving

Giving is supposed to be a supreme act of human goodness, and so it is, but it's no crime to receive. On the contrary, receiving is essential, because it takes two to make a gift—a giver and a receiver.

Receiving—plain, uncomplicated acceptance—is the nicest thing you can do for a giver, whether his offering is a present or hospitality, instruction or a service or an honor. Take it graciously; it's the most effective way on earth to say thank you.

Giving graciously

Every relationship in life is based on giving and receiving, from the purchase of a loaf of bread to treaties between nations, and unless it is so rooted, it soon dissolves. Without receiving there could be no trade or commerce, no government, law, education, manners, love.

Some people are wary of receiving because, they say, it obligates them to give in return, not so much a tangible object but their affection, interest, love. And love, they insist, is not to be commanded.

It's far easier to give than to receive graciously. If you doubt that, consider how you receive a compliment. Do you regard it with suspicion? Are you secretly pleased, and secretly ashamed of the pleasure? Do you deprecate yourself and try to turn it off on someone else? It is no small skill to receive well.

Receiving is not so much getting as taking, and there is a difference. Getting implies a certain aggression; taking is receptivity — to people, ideas, change, experience. An old saying runs, "A closed hand cannot receive," and neither can a closed mind.

The importance of receiving

A few days ago, a friend, a young mother with no money to spare, called me long distance just to say she missed me. Her call came at a moment when I needed cheering, and when the three minutes were up, my impulse was to say to the operator, "Reverse the charges and let us talk." But I caught myself in time. What a way to receive a gift! It would have been like saying, "I can afford this and you can't." Instead I said good-by and mailed off a note to tell her how much I had enjoyed her call.

I'm learning, I hope, to accept what people give me and let it enrich my life, and theirs. So much is said about the importance of giving that we often forget the equal necessity of receiving.

Love vs. Courtesy

I do not believe in applying love, like a mustard plaster, to the world's woes. I am extremely wary of brotherhood, and if I am asked to love the whole human race, I confess I am unequal to the task. Love, in my somewhat limited experience, is a one-to-one exchange that rules out clump relationships. People who would embrace large numbers of their fellow-men often are incapable of loving one singular person at close range. Diffused affection is less demanding than specific involvement.

What the world needs is not global love but global courtesy, that easy, settled goodwill that can listen to almost anything without losing its temper or its self-confidence. I didn't make up that phrase. It was taught to me by the poet Robert Frost, and he used it as a measure of true education. Love might pity a hungry man; courtesy would feed him. Love makes excuses for faults; courtesy, without condemning, demands standards. Love is provincialism; it wants to make the world over in its own image; it says, "We have piped unto you, and ye have not danced." Courtesy takes the universe as given, pipes for its own delight, and lets who will dance.

What I Have Learned From Other People's Children

Like many people without children of their own, I have strong opinions about them. Unlike some, I am blessed with an assortment of friends between two and twenty who are busily engaged in shattering my opinions and remaking them. We seem to be surviving.

One of the most constricting notions adults superimpose on children is that they give meaning to life. Ought we not to be reassuring *them* on this point—that life is worth living? A teen-age boy said to me, "Dad says the reason he's worked so hard all his life is us kids. Jeepers! How's that supposed to make us feel?" Children are not ornaments or possessions by which to measure our success or importance. If we find they add meaning to life, that is our privilege and our problem, not theirs.

I sometimes think we owe it to the young to be wrong—to have ideas and be wrong. A child desperately needs a world where people believe in something, value something, hope something, hold something. He needs a three-dimensional world he can walk around in without falling off. Most adults would not dream of tossing a child into the sea to find out whether he could swim, but we do it spiritually all the time, and children resent this almost more than physical cruelty because they cannot comprehend it.

Another outrage we inflict on children is to blunt their critical awareness. Most of the time we do it without knowing it, but that only compounds the felony. Developed critical judgment is almost the whole goal and definition of education; yet adults consistently stifle it in children, all the while prating of teaching them to "think for themselves" and urging them to be creative, by which is meant pasting things up. . . .

Four things to remember

If I had children, of course, I should make mistakes (I make them even without children of my own), but there are four things I would try to remember. (1) I would maintain my own ways and identity, partly as a means of helping the child attain his own. No mature person asks another to gratify his need for person-ness or justify his reasons for living. (2) I would *listen* to him, not only to what he said but to what he did not say and to what he meant. He could not always command my attention, but when he had it, it would be his fully. (3) I would take the child seriously—not the relationship to me, but himself. This would mean respecting his separateness and affording him the same privacy, dignity, courtesy and right to opinion I owe all other human beings. (4) Above all, I would be all my selves with him—not only parent but friend, citizen, opponent, person sometimes wrong, writer with a professional world apart. I remember vividly the day I discovered my mother was a woman first, before she belonged to me or anyone else. I was fourteen and the memory can still make me catch my breath. I felt surprised, enlightened, alive, linked forever to womankind through all the ages. It forms a shining strand between us today.

No adult can ever really enter the world of children. We are shut out by the laws of living and must accept it with good grace. But they must someday live in our world. It is our task to make it real, attractive, powerful, worth growing up into. We do it by minding our own business and sometimes reaching out a hand. I did not make that up. I was taught it by other people's children.

What Have I Learned From Men?

I owe to the teaching and example of men many of the most precious things I know: how to swim and dance and kindle a fire; that the split seconds of eternity are now; what aloneness is—and to like it.

Men know as women do not that it is not only possible to love more than one person at a time, it is inescapable. Love is not solely marriage and family life. It is the ability to get inside another person's head—"to walk a mile in his moccasins," the Indians say—so that his sensibilities become yours for just a while. Love is awareness.

From the men I have loved I have learned some patience and courage, and the immense lesson of nonpossession without which no relationship—between men and women, between friends of the same sex, between adults and children—is wholly genuine.

From men who have loved me I have learned that love has a thousand faces, each to be recognized and cherished for what it is.

Taking a risk

Men have taught me the mighty requirement of risking my life occasionally. I am not talking about the body that enwraps my breath—though that too—but the habits, customs, judgment and beliefs that make up much of what I call me. Women, with their nesting instinct, can be all too willing to exchange the great possibilities for the small, grubby, sure thing. Men are better at taking a risk than women are.

This is not to argue danger for danger's sake; only a neurotic or a professional stunt man does that. But we need to remember that dignity comes from daring, not dullness, and growth from roaming beyond the arbitrary landmarks of the soul.

It is men I have to thank for showing me the significance of money. Women are creatures of extremes. Because we are quick to perceive spiritual values and we know instinctively that money can't buy everything, we leap rashly to the other absolute—the belief that the best things in life are free. This is wrong headed.

Money is toil, talent and production, and to scorn or misuse it is to scorn or misuse the sources from which it springs. Men respect money because they pay a price for it in time, thought and energy. A woman often wants it accumulated in one place as though the only safe place for it were behind bars. Actually, this is not so. Economy is not parsimony, it is management. You have to spend to live; wisdom lies in spending skillfully. . . .

Men are not so very different

More than all else I have learned from men that underneath the man-exterior required by society there lies a being not so very different from myself. There is altogether too much division of humanity into male and female, mine and thine, this and the other. Men are people. They too dream and care, hope and pray, laugh and wonder what others think of them. They hurt, labor, cry and doubt and they do it all inside where it imposes burdens on nobody but themselves. They are buffeted by a world they neither always understand nor relish any better than women do, and somehow they manage to leave most of it outside on the mat like a Dutchman's shoes when they come home.

I like men. I do not half remember the lessons they have taught me at the times I need them most, but through them I keep learning to be a better woman and thus what it means to be a whole person. And I thank them. And I'm glad.

Cherishing His Privacy— And Yours

Never to be quite alone is one of the rich gains of marriage . . . and, paradoxically, one of its grave losses. Every healthy human spirit needs both love and, if you will, loneliness. There is nothing dark and frightening about this. On the contrary, privacy is a kind of mercy that lets love stay alive.

Any man who is a man insists upon his own experience with the world—that is, to go on being a man, a self. It's all that can be loved. Nobody can love a nothing.

At one time a measure of privacy was inherent in a man's work—ploughing, riding fence, seafaring, blacksmithing. Storekeepers and teachers walked alone to work, or rode a horse; doctors and clergymen spent solitary hours in their buggies making calls. Even in cities men went home to midday dinner and an hour's uninterrupted repose. I can remember my grandfather lying down after lunch with a clean black sock over his eyes. The one word he had for us children was "Scat!" I marveled at this, being of an age to hate daytime naps, but when I asked him about it, he told me, "I don't always sleep; I just lie still and invite my soul."

In the pulse and urgency of modern industrial life —on commuter trains and congested highways, in office, plant, suburb, classroom, apartment—privacy has all but vanished. Sometimes it is so remote people lose track of what it is that's missing and only feel a vague unease. It is a wise wife who takes account of this and provides emotional breathing space for her husband, for her children, and not least, for herself.

A sense of independent being

Preoccupation with the urgency of "interpersonal relationships" easily persuades us to believe that human beings exist exclusively in a context. An immortal soul is widely discredited, and even a mind or personality is said to be only a bundle of reactions. We seem to ourselves to be somebody, but this, say some experts, is a mild delusion, harmless if not taken too seriously. But any reticence, any reluctance to lay bare every thought or feeling is suspicious. "If he won't talk about it, something is wrong," is the current dictum. This is not the place for philosophical fine points, but whether or not the self exists, the fact remains that men and women are not satisfied without a sense of independent being. Instinctively, we love those who support that sense, and we resist furiously whoever tramples on it. Lack of privacy destroys spontaneous intimacy. If one has to fight for his identity, he will protect it by throwing up more barricades and no-trespassing signs than he needs.

Geography alone—what we might call structural privacy—is by no means the whole of it. There is a subtler requirement of keeping one's hands off and one's nose out—mentally and emotionally—*when the situation calls for it.* The goal is not total indifference, but love does not mean total occupation like a regiment of Marines, either. The essence of physical privacy is not having to explain, to others or even to oneself.

The secret self

The secret self within the man you love is not your enemy but your greatest friend and ally—if you make it clear that you are not opposed to it. In large societies, relationships have to be standardized and personality suppressed. That's why an army has codes and regulations; otherwise there would be chaos. Only in the one-to-one intensity of love is there freedom, individuality, privacy. Cherish it.

What Do We Owe Our Parents?

One of my friends is a confused, unhappy person whose mother, in desperation, once cried to me, "Where did I fail?"

I maintain that she didn't. She has two other children, one happily married, the other doing brilliant work in his field. "Do you claim full credit for their achievements?" I asked.

She was indignant. "Certainly not."

"Then why hold yourself completely to blame for your other daughter's troubles?" She looked at me oddly. She wanted to believe me, but I doubt that she did. Such is the climate of current—and supposedly enlightened — opinion that both she and her daughter are dedicated to the notion of wholesale parental responsibility for whatever goes wrong in children's lives.

Of course, parents make mistakes, but they also do many things well. Perspective, judgment, taste, restraint, the humanities, law ethics, love—these too are taught-and-learned lessons. We did not in our infant wisdom pluck them out of thin air. They were taught to us first by our parents. And it is high time we balanced this fact against any legitimate grievances we might have.

We owe them breathing space

Parents may be honest in maintaining that we do not owe them money, but what of attitudes, appreciation, understanding? Many insist that these, too, are in no way owed. But here there is a frightening gap between what they say and what they mean.

As one father put it airily, "Oh, that's taken for granted, that my children love me and want me around. That's not a question of 'owe.'"

My own mother, who is as practical in most ways as anyone I've ever known, said, "I suppose I hoped we'd have enough in common to be friends."

We owe our parents breathing space—room to move around and even to make drastic changes in their lives, if they wish, to change their line of work or remarry.

A man in his late fifties visited in our home last year. After years in the business world, he had been offered a teaching post in a small college and had accepted it. When he spoke of what he hoped to accomplish in his teaching, his eyes shone.

We asked him what his children thought and he threw up his hands. "I don't think they've quite accepted it yet," he said, with a chuckle. "It meant selling our old house, of course, and all the kids could think of was where they'd go for Christmas. Oh, they don't mean to be selfish, but I sometimes think children are the ones who are stuffy."

We owe them acceptance as people

What if our parents are the kind of people we would never choose as friends? That happens, and it is best to recognize it. Having done so, we owe them a few fundamental decencies.

We owe them patience: wait a few years. It is quite common for parents to like their children better at certain ages than at others, but they do not abandon them in off-seasons. . . .

Most of all we owe our parents what we owe ourselves or anyone else: an acceptance as people. Right, wrong, impatient, generous, serene, suspicious—old people are, as a wise woman once said to me, "just like young people, only more so." It gave me pause for I will be there myself one day.

Marriage and Martyrdom

Most modern young women have been nurtured from the crib on the theory of personal fulfillment as a right and a necessity, not only in marriage but in life. Their husbands, while bred on the same ideal, are better able to tolerate not finding it in marriage, since their work or side interests open other opportunities. Wives, then, sometimes resort to martyrdom.

The tradition of male dominance

To be a martyr is to die for a great cause. A wife who affects martyrdom as a style of life, while very much breathing, and still with us, is a plain fraud. Such behavior withers and kills husbandly love because it parades before the world how paltry and worthless that love is. The phony martyr cries: "Look how little I get in exchange for my endurance, my service, my sacrifice. Look how I suffer, and for what?" How can love expand and blossom under such blackmail?

Although a man may sometimes be a martyr, women fall into the state much more readily, perhaps partly because of their lingering subservient position. While not as clear-cut as it used to be, the tradition of male dominance hovers in the fringes. And martyrdom is one way of resisting masculine tyranny, real or fancied. The self-anointed martyr's objective is to make her partner feel guilty of having inflicted a grievous wrong—a wrong that usually exists only in the martyr's mind. It is a foolish objective, for the husband who feels guilty will usually end up by blaming his wife for his suffering. Guilt is the poisoner of love. . . .

Examining life goals

Any fiancée who regards her approaching wifehood as a severe sacrifice had better think twice about marrying. On the other side, a man shouldn't assume that his future wife has merely dabbled in some interest because, up till now, she hasn't had him. He is surely setting her—and himself—up for martyrdom. A gifted young woman photographer told her husband-to-be categorically that he could take her with cameras, or not at all. "I figured," she said, "the world was full of girls who would give up everything if that was the sort of woman he wanted." And he was appalled by the thought of a wife who expected him "to do her living for her," as he put it. So they married happily. This doesn't mean all wives want careers. It means a couple should examine what exactly a girl does want from life over the long haul and be prepared to accommodate it.

Fulfillment is a private endeavor

We should laugh at expecting marriage to make one well-read or open-minded, rich and befriended, appreciative of music and art, or politically-informed. Yet this is exactly what is demanded when partnership is equated with total satisfaction. Love may be one kind of answer to the mystery of living, but with marriage new questions arise. True, there are now two of you asking them—but that's all. Oscar Wilde said a thing does not become true because a man dies for it. So, too, love is not great just because one sacrifices all else for it. There is no worse testimonial to love than martyrdom and nothing more suffocating. You probably cannot escape the American impulse toward personal fulfillment, and there is no proof that it is false. But fulfillment is, and should be, private endeavor, in or out of marriage. It is not easy to carry the dead weight of another person, and any sane man will eventually quit trying. If that is what you want—be a martyr.

Is Success
A Dirty Word?

Success is as obsolete as a buttonhook. Once the great American dream, it has slowly wheeled around to become the great American bugbear. The fashionable thing is to cry down success as neurotic in origin, selfish in pursuit, doomed to disappointment in the end.

I asked a group of students why they planned to work in their various fields and they replied, "To make me more interesting as a person"; "So I can give my family the important things of life"; "To keep myself well-rounded." Not one of them said the field itself absorbed or excited him. Some of them talked of "making a contribution," but what exactly they could not say; and no one said he simply wanted to be the best historian or journalist or lawyer in the world.

I don't quite believe they didn't want it—but they thought it best not to say so, or to call it by some other name. . . .

Success isn't a monster

We resist success because we don't know exactly what it is. We think of it as a mysterious something which some people have, others go after by vicious means, and still others miss through no fault of their own. It is not that obscure. Success is the culmination of endeavor, whether it is directed toward achieving an atomic chain reaction or making a dress; digging up ancient cities or learning to ski.

Success isn't a perennial holiday, nor does it always look pretty. It is dedication to purpose and lifelong attention to that ideal. Whether the ideal is important is a matter of taste and experience and is not of itself a measure of success. Because you do not wish to attain proficiency as an actor or an astrophysicist, it does not follow that anyone who does is foolish.

People sometimes say punctiliously that success has nothing to do with money, when what they mean is that it isn't necessarily marketable, which of course is true. But success *is* usually visible, because you can no more bottle it up than you can bottle sunlight. If you do whatever you do well—make a pie or drive a car or play the piano—people around you will know it and frequently say so in one coin or another.

Success isn't a monster that consumes our talents; it is the art of living with those talents—and living implies continuity, progression, evolution. The very word "succeed" means one thing following another. Success isn't a single peak of achievement, it's a whole mountain range.

The reward will be more to do

At the same time, success is inside your head; it's a feeling. Eleanor Roosevelt . . . often told how she overcame her timidity and self-doubt by pretending to be self-assured and poised—not faking it, but assuming it as she might put on a dress—until these became her nature.

If success is fleeting, so is life in a sense; and that doesn't mean either one was never worth having. To say, "I don't care to succeed," is really to say, "I don't expect anything," which is avoiding defeat by being defeated before you start.

Success is expectancy plus responsibility. [Responsibility] is much needed at all levels and it is so intrinsic to success that it won't leave you at one level. If you succeed at whatever you're doing today, the reward will be more to do tomorrow. In success there is no place to stop and some people find this disquieting. But the definition of succeeding—one thing following the next—is a pretty good working definition of life, and even of infinity.

Never Say Never!

Few people set out deliberately to miss the wonder and richness of living, but it is treacherously easy to do. A postponement here, a side-stepping there, a retreat elsewhere—and behold, a life dried up behind a wall of negatives: "I can't"; "I won't"; "It could never happen."

Out of curiosity, I kept for a week a list of all the "nevers" and similar denials I heard myself and others say. It was much too long to repeat here, but some of them were these: I would never be a working mother; I'll never marry outside my religion; I can never balance my checkbook—I'm not good at figures; I never do volunteer work; I never wear pink; I won't have a dishwasher in the house; I won't color my hair; I never go to big parties; I'll never marry a career woman; I'll never speak to him again; I can't stand jazz.

I know a brilliant, famous woman who has led a fascinating and rewarding life—so far, as she likes to remind me—and once I asked her if she could select from her variegated years a single most important lesson learned—so far. She was silent a moment and then said, "Yes. That all the things you think can never happen, will happen. And all the things you think you'll never do, you will probably do."

Life is that which flows

"Never" is a cunning thief that impoverishes the spirit. We are all born to unspecified possibilities. They are ahead of us, waiting. What starts out as a simple recognition of fact too often digs in as a practice and a principle, and the possibilities narrow and stop. To say, "I have never been to Europe," is harmless if regrettable, but the moment it becomes, "I never go to Europe" and "I never will go," we are being robbed under our very noses.

Stubbornly saying no to large and small ventures, we find ourselves in a circular trap. Like two-year-old children who scream "No!" at the world even when they mean yes, we at once defend and resent our negations, until we scarcely know what we want or need.

The world is wide, and complicated. Without preferences and rejections, there would be no personality. Without some boundaries to give pattern to life, every minor decision would become a major crisis; whether to come or go; whether to act or wait; whether to speak or keep still.

But never?

Plainly, some negatives are suitable and necessary.

At a certain age, one can rightly say, "I never wear makeup"—or high heels, or mink coats. In certain circumstances, it makes sense to say, "I cannot spend more than ten dollars for this." But any position, no matter how wise and rustproof at the time, may be outgrown, for life by definition is that which flows, moves, evolves, changes.

A negative can become a positive

According to Webster, "never" means not only time but degree. When we say, "Never fear" or "Never mind," we do not mean indefinitely in time but in no degree, none at all. So, in reverse, to cast off your negatives does not mean wallowing or being blown about heedlessly by every whim, but to put aside by degrees those negations that have become or always were frightened, indifferent, habitual, or suspicious; to listen; to try.

It is quite possible that the fragments and segments of our lives are related in some unified way, so that the thing we say so flatly we will never do is the very thing that some other portion of us needs for completion. That is why the effort to break out of the pattern exhilarates us; it is a creative act. A negative reversed becomes a positive.

If you would make yourself felt in the world and known to yourself, say yes to life. Never say never— or perhaps it should be: rarely say it.

Change Means Fulfillment

It is plain to anyone with half a mind to look that all life is change—action, events, evolution, what the social scientists call on-going. Inertia is not life but death, and change ought to be as comfortable to us as breathing. By refusing to change, we limit the availability of our own possibilities, to ourselves, to our friends, and to the world.

The longing for something to endure is illogical but understandable, and it infects all human creatures. Children and young people are supposed to welcome change, but that seems to me unfounded, though, like adults, they vary in their capacity to receive it. Watch a six-year-old clinging to his mother on the first day of school, or a girl weeping dramatically over leaving her friends when the family moves to a new city, and you realize how deep and innate is hostility to the new. The words "forever" and "always" recur in children's stories and young love songs, in adult prayers and ceremonies, like an incantation against tomorrow.

Thus we all seek to impress ourselves on events

and time, and to make life an establishment. The desire for permanence is universal, but the curious fact is it can be fulfilled only by yielding to its fancied opposite: change.

There is a time to let go of the incidental baggage of the past, however well it has served us, and to take up the accoutrements of the present. If you ask me how to tell when this time comes, I can only answer that I do not know. Nobody does. It varies for each of us with our nature and the hundred thousand circumstances of our separate lives. It helps, perhaps, to cultivate the early realization that change not only is coming but is here, an ingredient of every day we live—and happily so. It is not change that defeats us but monotony. The necessary art is not, heaven forbid, to "grow old gracefully," but simply to grow; to see oneself as a developing creature, rather than a static one. What becomes of anyone is the mystery and wonder and necessity of life.

A changing self-concept

One day my sister and I were working in her kitchen when her twelve-year-old son asked, "Mother, just who is Adolf Hitler, anyway?" We looked at each other, unbelieving, and before answering him, my sister said softly to me, "Well, we made it. We're the older generation." Startling thought after twenty years of pinning that label on somebody else. Of course, neither of us was old, only old*er* in relation to the child, and that was the whole point.

Change demands a constant reordering of one's *concept* of oneself, which is not easy, but it brings with it the reward of understanding.

Life is never settled

I was interviewing a group of bright, attractive college girls on the subject of woman and her special goals, and I found they had a very realistic concept of themselves for the next five or six years—as wives, housekeepers, mothers of young children. But when I asked what they expected to do for challenge and adventure at thirty, or forty, they were not only blank, they were offended. One girl finally said, "Me? Forty? Don't be silly, I can't even imagine it." Another replied, "I'll face that when I get to it," and a third remarked, "Oh, well, by that time you've had it. Life is settled."

Is it, indeed? Life is never settled, nor should it be. Life is endless choice, perpetual discovery, constant revision of all you thought you knew.

Life holds out to each of us the promise of becoming whatever we have in us to become. To change is not only to fulfill our own promise but to transform life itself, to make one's own contribution to the sum of what life is—and that is not to live in vain.

A Word About Values

We are suspended in language, which is a swift and powerful shorthand for communicating enormous chunks of reality; and it is easy to fail in love with the shorthand, thinking that by saying the word, we have invoked the reality beneath. We say the word "love" and expect others to swoon; we say the words "truth" or "patriotism," and everyone is supposed to stand up tall, with a glint in his eye. "Value" is only a word for which we invent and discover meanings —plural, more than one, for values grow as we grow, change as we change, contract only if we contract. The very atoms of our bodies . . . the air around us are in perpetual, high-speed, dazzling motion. To be alive at all is to move, act, do, become. To use a system of values as a means of holding life still is a sleepwalking state.

Values by themselves are no guarantee of goodness or happiness. They can be used blindly to hide from life. Parents sometimes say they know their children will make mistakes, but please let them not be the same mistakes that they, the parents, made. Why not? Such mistakes have served mankind for centuries in the growing-up process. We all made more or less the same blunders in learning to walk, and cried because they hurt; but nobody argues that we ought to omit them and be carried in somebody else's arms for the rest of our lives.

It is equally monstrous if the *spirit* never tries to walk upright and alone. I am not suggesting, of course, that you rush out and plunge into every vagrant experience life offers. Wallowing will only blunt your sensibilities, not heighten them. I am saying that living is daring, trying, being wrong and trying again, going beyond where you were last year —but it is not anarchy. Without a present sense of values, you have no base to push off from, and you can't get somewhere from nowhere. Start with the values you now have, and live by them as far as they will take you. I promise you, with all my heart, the day will come when they fail, and then you will know it is time to re-examine your beliefs.

The direct tang of being

Don't cheat the self that is waiting to be. To enlarge your values is wisdom; to throw them out is suicide—spiritual and sometimes physical.

As a fellow human being, I urge upon you a strong sense of values, not as a formula for happiness or success—but as the only way I know to participate in what the American philosopher Ernest Hocking has called "the direct tang of being"; so that one day, when you look back, you will have lived, and you will know it.

About the Author—
By the Author

Although my name is Michael Drury, I am a woman, not, please note, a girl. I was a girl once, but I like to think I have outgrown that. My parents anticipated that I would be a boy and tried to swing a little prenatal influence by calling me Mike prior to my actual debut on earth. Subsequent efforts were made to amend the name, but nothing ever quite adhered except Mike, and eventually Michael. (The Biblical female spelling is *Michal*, but I discovered this too late to change it.)

I was born in northern California and grew up amid redwood trees and wine vineyards with apple and prune orchards in between. It was lovely country to grow up in. I spent the first twelve years of my life in a tree, and close to the land and sea, the Russian River, Indians, animals, fish, canoes, campfires and storytellers, county fairs, small-town politics and western tradition, cattle ranching, sheep, and Spanish haciendas. This to a writer is riches, for people are his business. Words are but a means of communicating with, from, to and about people.

My family was largely composed of newspaper people, and they hated to get out of bed—all except me. I was a rebel in that respect. They taught me to write leads when I was still in school so that when the fire siren blew at night I could exercise my foolish romantic notions by getting up to chase the fire. I attended public schools (schools which I now know were surprisingly good) until college, when I went to Stanford University, from which I was graduated in 1940. I wrote radio commercials in San Francisco for a time and then put down $53.83 for a one-way, coach train ticket to New York where my quarry was—publishers. When I got out at the other end in Pennsylvania Station I had $20, a portable typewriter, a portable radio, and hope. I had never been east of the Sierra Nevada, but in college I had mastered two crafts the twentieth century could not get along without—I was a good waitress and a good switchboard operator. I knew I could eat. I have also cooked for a living twice, and I now regard that as a kind of social security. One thing to be said for cooks: they always eat.

I served an apprenticeship on the editorial staffs of three magazines: *Life*, *Harper's* and *McCall's*, in that order, and acquired a second college education.

Among other things, what these magazines gave me was the same kind of association with good minds that the university had given me—less academic of course, but equally instructive. I have been blessed with good teachers and good bosses. I recently told a corporation audience that bosses aren't so bad; they can lick you into full capacity, and anybody who does that is a good thing, no matter how rough the going.

In 1947 I began to free-lance full time, and have earned my living at it ever since. I have sold some 300 articles, stories, short novels and poems to the major national magazines, and a few not-so-major ones. I stayed in New York 27 years, married a Navy officer during World War II, and now live alone (with a large red cat) in a New England seacoast town. Like Robert Frost, about whom I once wrote a biographical article, I am fortunate enough to have my vocation and my avocation as one. When I am not writing, I sail a little, walk, read voraciously, cook, make jam and jelly, go to concerts, garden a little, swim, talk to people, ride my bicycle, prowl around New England. I move around in the United States quite a lot, too. It's a big country, and unless one touches base in it here and there, he forgets what America really is.

Michael Drury

Set in Weiss Roman, a typeface designed
by Emil Rudolf Weiss for the Bauer Type Foundry.
Headings and titles hand set in Elizabeth,
a style created by Miss E. Friedländer, a pupil of Weiss.
Printed on Hallmark Eggshell Book paper.
Edited by Barbara Loots.
Book design by Susan Howey.